CORETTA'S JOURNEY

The Life and Times of Coretta Scott King

Alice Faye Duncan

Illustrated by
R. Gregory Christie

CALKINS CREEK
AN IMPRINT OF ASTRA BOOKS FOR YOUNG READERS
New York

Struggle is a never-ending process.
Freedom is never really won.
You earn it and win it in every generation.
—**Coretta Scott King**

Introduction

Listen to Coretta Scott King in any recorded interview. Notice that her speech is lyrical and measured like music. It is for this reason that I wrote her biography as a collection of poetry and prose. I wanted to capture the musical quality of her voice and bearing. The poetry forms in this book include acrostics, free verse, haiku, and tanka poems. Make time to write your own poetry. Use your words to celebrate the people in history who inspire you, to pursue freedom and justice for all.

Contents

1927

Alabama soil
A fertile plain of black earth
Coretta was born . . .

This Bitter Earth

The baby-child left her planet in the heavens on a streak of light. She spirited past stars and moons to have her blooming in Heiberger, Alabama. It was love that set Coretta's soul in flight and picked her earthbound destination. Love gave her a home in the arms of Bernice and Obadiah Scott. The Scotts gave Coretta two siblings. Big sister Edythe was born in 1924 and baby brother Obie Junior was born in 1930.

Could any good thing come from Heiberger? It was a tiny segregated town, ten miles east from the city of Marion in north Perry County. Farmland and pine forests covered the area, far as the eye could see. The Scott family owned hundreds of acres.

Land and money did not protect them. Blacks in Heiberger lived under the weight of slavery's past. They suffered daily attacks of racial injustice and endured Jim Crow laws that required Black people to enter side doors and sit in the back of buses and trains.

Coretta learned a bitter lesson as she grew into girlhood. Racial segregation made black skin a prison of second-class citizenship. Coretta lived the struggle. White students in Perry County went to school for nine months a year, while Black students received only five months of school. White students rode to school on a big yellow bus, while Coretta, her siblings, and Black classmates walked three miles to Crossroads, a one-room school, filled with one hundred children and two Black teachers.

When Crossroads School was in session, small black feet plodded dirt roads in the heat, rain, and snow. Coretta stepped high. She wanted to read at any cost.

However, the chains of segregation rattled her temper. Coretta was not an easygoing girl. She knuckle-punched classmates, cousins, and siblings who disagreed with her opinions. Edythe and Obie Junior would cry that Coretta was MEAN.

1937

Spunky spitfire girl
Long black hair and dark brown eyes
Looking toward Heaven
From the wooden mourners' bench
Asking God—*Who will I be?*

Blues girl like Bessie
Belting brokenhearted tunes
Dancing a shimmy
Around the old Victrola
Asking God—*Who will I be?*

Cotton-picking girl
Picking more pounds than a man
Climbing trees at night
Dream catcher and stargazer
Asking God—*Who will I be?*

Alabama Fire

Coretta's parents obeyed the cosmic pull of the planets. Obadiah Scott built Bernice McMurry a home with his bare hands in 1920. They married in 1921, when he was twenty-two and she was seventeen.

Coretta's parents were alike in many ways. They both came from Black families who owned farmland and pine forests in Perry County. Bernice farmed the family garden, managed the farm animals, and cared for the children. Obadiah was the first Black man in town to own a truck. He hauled lumber to surrounding sawmills during the week. Bernice and Obadiah taught themselves to cut hair and on Saturdays, they used their home as a barbershop. Neither parent graduated from high school, but they were wise and hardworking.

While Bernice loved Obie Senior with unwavering tenderness, she did not preach marriage. She told Coretta and Edythe, "Get an education and try to be somebody."

And while America was a male-dominated society where men lorded over women, Obadiah was different. He did not view his daughters as weaklings. He told Coretta and Edythe, "You can do anything anyone else can do."

White men resented Obadiah's can-do spirit and his majestic dignity. He never let his shoulders slump, but spoke with all men eye to eye.

In 1942 when Coretta was fifteen, white terrorists torched the family home on Thanksgiving night. The Scotts escaped unharmed, but the house Obadiah built with his hands burned to a heap of ashes. For several days, Coretta cried over the loss of clothes, photographs, and her collection of Bessie Smith blues records.

Obadiah stood over the ashes and announced to his family, "We don't have time to cry." He wiped their tears. Then he said a prayer, asking God to forgive the evildoers.

Forgiveness was slow to reach Coretta. She stewed in anger as she studied her father's courage in the wake of the fire. He returned to work without bitterness and moved his family into a rented house. Over the next several years, Obadiah built a new home and saved enough money to purchase a local lumber mill.

Once again, malevolent men targeted Obadiah Scott because they despised his audacity to dream and achieve his goals. He had owned the mill for two weeks when a white logger asked to buy it. When Obadiah refused to sell, the logger served him a threat saying, "It will never do you any good." On the following Monday, arsonists torched the lumber mill and it burned to the ground.

The heap of rubble and torched dreams made Bernice Scott cautious. She did not trust whites in Perry County. As for Obadiah, sawmill embers filled him with a blazing conviction to build a grocery store adjacent to his new home. Faith fueled Obadiah's determination. Scott's Grocery Store welcomed Black and white customers. The new business succeeded and proved an important lesson to Bernice and her children. Coretta said it often, "My father was one of the most fearless men I've ever met."

1945

Lincoln School received Coretta in 1939 during her seventh-grade year.
It was a "Negro school" in Marion founded by missionaries after the Civil War.
Negro teachers worked beside white teachers, like the progressive pair,
Cecil and Fran Thomas, who gave Coretta a new worldview of possibility.
On no occasion did they humiliate the child like white folks in her past.
Lincoln also gave Coretta a vivacious voice teacher in Olive J. Williams.
Negro girls emulated the Negro woman's poise and diction.

School polished pugnacious Coretta Scott into a glimmering black pearl.
Coretta shined. She studied voraciously and graduated valedictorian—1945.
Her sister Edythe set the example. She graduated Lincoln valedictorian—1943.
Obadiah and Bernice scrimped and saved to raise money for school supplies.
Obadiah turned his truck into a makeshift bus to drive Negro students to Lincoln.
Lincoln served freedom on a plate. Books are freedom. Coretta wanted more.

Jim Crow Ohio

Coretta inherited gumption from her mother. Like Uranus, the rare planet that rotates on its side, Bernice Scott bucked traditional patterns to follow her own path. She was the first woman in Heiberger to drive a car and lumber truck in the 1920s.

As for appearances, it seemed to the naked eye that Bernice was Obadiah Scott's opposite. He was short and black like coffee. Bernice was a tall Black woman the color of cream. Together, they raised their children to be independent thinkers. The Scotts encouraged Coretta and her siblings to voice their ideas at the dinner table and to develop their personal interests to establish professional hopes and dreams.

Big sister Edythe loved books and traveled up North with the Lincoln Little Chorus to sing and raise money for school. After one concert at Antioch College in Yellow Springs, Ohio, the faculty offered Edythe a scholarship. She entered Antioch in 1943 as America assailed Hitler's Germany in World War II.

Ohio appeared to be Alabama's opposite. Up North, there were no Jim Crow signs for Blacks to take back seats or enter side doors. Antioch College did not practice segregation. Blacks and Asians lived on campus with the majority white students. Everyone sat in the same classrooms. All students were served in the same dining hall. Coretta wanted equality. She followed Edythe to Antioch on scholarship in 1945.

Antioch's Black student body grew from three to six when Coretta reached Yellow Springs. Leaving the limitations of the South spirited her into a new galaxy.

She befriended Christians, Muslims, Buddhists, and Jews. Politics and pacifism captured her interests. She sang a new song—opera. And while rigorous college classes challenged her mettle, Coretta announced to Edythe, she would make her "best better."

As Coretta toiled over books, she made time to meet with friends. They discussed anti-war initiatives and political strategies to eliminate segregation and voter suppression in the American South. While she studied up North, love for her people down home was strong. How could she shine her light to make them proud?

With help from her Antioch music teacher Walter Anderson, Coretta honed her soprano voice. Like Paul Robeson, a famous concert artist who broke racial barriers singing around the globe, she prayed to follow Robeson's star. Unfortunately, Antioch did not offer a music degree and Coretta resorted to a diploma in elementary education. If singing opera failed, it was her plan to change America—one classroom at a time.

Obadiah's baby girl encountered dark clouds in college. Sister Edythe left Antioch in 1947 to finish her studies at Ohio State, fifty miles away. Baby sister felt abandoned. To make matters worse, racism showed its face. Yellow Springs denied Coretta a chance to practice teach in the white public schools because she was Black.

Coretta took action. She met with the Antioch president to report the injustice. He encouraged her to practice teach at the all-Black school in Xenia, Ohio. NO! Coretta would not submit to the segregation of her past. She tried to rally Antioch teachers and students to support her. When they all turned away, she waged a one-woman appeal to the local school board.

Coretta wrote in her petition that America's "inner corruption cannot long persist without backfiring."

With no one left to help champion her case, she stayed true to her conviction. Coretta did not go to Xenia, but accepted a second option. She taught in the Antioch campus school to qualify for her teaching certificate. Graduation day arrived in 1951. With confidence Coretta marched onward to pave uncharted roads.

1951

Horace Mann conceived the idea of free public schools.
He was the first president of Antioch College in 1853.
Mann motivated Coretta with his famous last words.
Antioch chiseled those words in stone.
Coretta scribbled them in a book.

"Be ashamed to die until
You have won
Some victory for humanity."

What victory and prize would Coretta achieve?
With only a few dollars in her pocketbook,
She boarded a train to study music in Boston.

Coretta entered the New England Conservatory in 1951.
Leaves shimmered red and gold like Venus.
It was September when she arrived.

The challenge of change stoked her fire.
Coretta prepared her soul to sing.

What Mama Said

"Get an education and try to be somebody."

Bernice Scott spoke these words to Coretta and Edythe across the seasons of girlhood. When Coretta was a young woman at Boston's New England Conservatory, the words sounded in her ears like rushing waves on the sea. It was an urgent call. *Get an education and try to be somebody.*

As she survived on crackers with peanut butter and worked part-time as a file clerk, music school prepared Coretta for center stage. She hoped to be the first Black vocalist to sing leading arias at New York's Metropolitan Opera. Coretta studied voice with the Metropolitan star Marie Sundelius to make this dream a reality.

Although money was scarce and winter in Boston seemed like endless weeks of snow and ice, Coretta did not waver from her dream to sing. Then without warning, there was a fluttering disruption. Mary Powell, a classmate at the conservatory, gave Coretta's phone number to a young Baptist preacher from Atlanta, Georgia. His name was Martin Luther King Jr. He was a theology student in the doctoral program at Boston University.

It was January 1952. Coretta told Mary, she did not want to be a preacher's wife.

Coretta liked music, dancing, and engaging conversations about American politics. From her childhood experience in Alabama, she was a Methodist, who considered Baptist preachers to be narrow-minded, loud, and boring. When Martin called to invite Coretta to lunch, she accepted. There was no giddiness. She knew this first date with Martin would also be the last. It was not. Gravitational pull rearranged her plans.

Martin drove to the conservatory in his green Chevrolet. Coretta was not impressed with his small stature or clean-shaven face. Without a mustache, he looked like a young boy. But when they entered Sharaf's Cafeteria and exchanged ideas over lunch, comfort and joy rested around their shoulders. The two shared similar views. They both despised poverty, racism, and war. Coretta planned to sing and use her voice to integrate American concert halls. Martin made plans to preach. He wanted to use his voice to destroy segregation with fiery sermons about justice and equal rights.

Coretta mesmerized Martin during lunch. He admired her sharp mind and long black hair. On the drive home, he said, "You have everything I have ever wanted in a wife."

Coretta asked incredulously, "What is that?"

Martin replied, "Character, intelligence, personality, and beauty."

As they went on other dates, Coretta discovered Martin was more than a gifted scholar and preacher. He danced a mean jitterbug at college socials and birthday parties.

In a letter to Edythe, Coretta wrote, "There is something about him that grows on you."

Coretta married Martin on June 18, 1953. The wedding took place in Alabama on her parents' lawn. Martin's father, Reverend Daddy King, officiated. At Coretta's request, Daddy King deleted words like "obey" and "submit" from the wedding vows.

Get an education and try to be somebody.

Coretta earned her music degree. Martin earned his doctorate. While it was easiest for Black college graduates to stay up North and succeed without the overt restrictions of segregation, the Kings left Boston in 1954. They followed a cosmic calling—faint to the ear. The green Chevy headed south for Montgomery, Alabama.

1955

Coretta Scott King
Martin Luther King Jr.
Venus and Saturn
A convergence of planets
A cosmic union of fate

Coretta Scott King
A songbird and preacher's wife
Dexter Baptist Church
Dr. King preached like Moses
Chattered Montgomery folks

Mrs. Rosa Parks
A nonviolent activist
Stubborn like granite
Arrested for her protest
When she took a front bus seat

Fierce winds of progress
Swept across Montgomery
Jim Crow squawked at death
Black folks put on walking shoes
Boycotted city buses

Dr. King stood up
Fanned the flames on Jim Crow's pyre
Fiery-tongued preacher
Pretty wife and newborn child
His family soon a target

BOOM! King's home was bombed
The bus boycott carried on
Fifty thousand strong
Black maids walked in snow and rain
December to December

BOOM! King's home was bombed
Coretta and baby cried
Martin grew fearful
Said—*Go to your father's house*
Coretta refused to leave

Obadiah Scott
Said—*Come home to Heiberger*
Coretta said—*NO*
Venus and Saturn converged
It was not a time to run

Bernice understood
Coretta was Obie's seed
Fireproof heart of faith
Baptized in racial hatred
A woman born for battle

Martin's Coretta
Venus and Saturn converged
Two agents for change
Marched down highways and bridges
Singing—*We shall not be moved*

The Movement

When Coretta lived in Montgomery, Rosa Parks stood as her paragon of womanhood. Rosa gave Coretta an example in protest and pluck when the Black seamstress challenged segregation on a city bus in 1955. While Rosa's actions inspired the Montgomery bus boycott, the boycott sparked the defining moment called the American Civil Rights Movement. For the next ten years, nonviolent protests like boycotts, sit-ins, and mass marches swept across the American South.

Nonviolence as a strategy to disarm legalized segregation in America was an idea whose time had come. Pacifist Bayard Rustin introduced Coretta to the philosophy of nonviolence when he lectured at Lincoln School in 1942. Dr. King read about nonviolent resistance and the Indian martyr Mahatma Gandhi during college. It was Gandhi's campaign of passive resistance that led to India's independence from British rule.

Coretta and Martin's textbook understanding of protest became flesh when segregationists bombed the Kings' home. Believing in the redemptive power of suffering, the Kings endured. They stayed in Montgomery until the boycott was victorious and the US Supreme Court outlawed segregation on American city buses in December 1956.

As the pastor of Montgomery's Dexter Baptist Church, Martin became a galvanizing voice during the boycott. His star rose over the city and Martin's popularity spread across the nation when his face appeared on the cover of *Time* magazine in 1957.

When a *Time* reporter asked about his strategy to

dismantle racial inequality in America, Martin replied, "The spirit of passive resistance came to me from the Bible and the teachings of Jesus. The techniques of execution came from Gandhi."

Two years after the boycott, Coretta and Martin were popular faces in the press. Dr. King was the leading voice of the Civil Rights Movement. In 1958 when he was twenty-nine, he wrote his first autobiography, *Stride Toward Freedom.*

Americans from all racial backgrounds and beliefs supported the Kings and their nonviolent philosophy. But, as witnessed in the Montgomery bombing, negative forces also tried to kill them. Not every opposing force was white and Southern.

Once, while Martin signed books in a New York City department store, an irrational Black woman stormed through the crowd. When Izola Curry was face-to-face with the leader, she hollered, "Luther King, I have been after you for five years." Then she pierced his chest with a letter opener.

Customers captured the woman and she was committed to an asylum for the mentally ill. As for Dr. King, he almost died. The blade pressed against his aorta and had to be surgically removed. Coretta cared for Martin's health. After three months of rest, the preacher, husband, and now father of two returned to the pulpit at Dexter Baptist Church.

Early in the movement, Coretta and Martin accepted the idea that believers in nonviolence do not repay evil with evil. They confront evil with faith and live by the conviction that suffering or death will ultimately yield equality and justice for all.

It was Dr. King's desire to live, but death did not frighten him. He told friends often that the "cosmic companionship" of God eased his fear in times of trouble. There was also one earthbound companion who boosted his confidence. Martin said it often: "Corrie, you are a brave soldier. I don't know what I would do without you."

1960

Coretta was not a swooning woman.
When hard times unloaded like a ton of bricks,
She did not flail her arms or wail for pity.
Placid waters possessed her inner constitution.
Coretta rocked steady in the middle of storms.
She comforted her children with bedtime stories.

The unflappable Coretta was tested in 1960.
Sounds of jangling jail keys and clanging cell doors
Spirited her soul into a posture of fervent prayer.
Martin sat in jail on countless occasions that year.
White segregationists serving as city police
Trailed his giant shadow wherever he marched.

When Coretta and Martin moved to Atlanta in 1960,
Black college students enlisted her husband's help.
The students railed against segregation and organized
Sit-in protests at downtown lunch counters.
Students were jailed and released—Dr. King was not.
A white judge sent Martin to the Reidsville penitentiary.

Coretta was pregnant with the couple's third child.
Her placid waters raged that tempestuous October.
The judge sentenced Martin four months on a chain gang.
The sentence was unjustified, cruel, and frightening.
Coretta closed her eyes to pray and the phone rang.
John F. Kennedy called—determined and ready to help.

Kennedy was a presidential candidate in 1960.
His opponent was Vice President Richard Nixon.
Coretta wanted her husband unchained and set free.
She explained how segregationists targeted Martin.
Kennedy's team appealed to the Georgia governor.
Martin was released and still—there was no peace.

The King children were badgered and bullied.
Mean boys called their daddy "jailbird!"
Dr. King threw his political weight behind JFK.
And Kennedy won the tight election in 1960.
Victory filled Coretta with hope for the future.
She huddled her children in a circle of hugs.

Called

It was 1963. Coretta now mothered four bright-eyed children: Yolanda, Marty, Dexter, and Bunny. It was Coretta's choice to be their mother. It was also her choice to march in anti-war demonstrations and travel to Switzerland in 1962. There she joined Women Strike for Peace in a rally to ban nuclear testing and end the Vietnam War, which had ravaged human life since 1955.

Motherhood and marching were challenges. But with help from Martin's sister, Christine, in Atlanta, Coretta organized her life around children and social justice.

Like every friendship and union, the Kings endured moments of disagreement. While Martin supported Coretta's drive for international peace, he wanted her satisfied serving in the home. Martin asked Coretta once, "You aren't totally happy being my wife and the mother of my children, are you?"

Coretta replied, "If that's all I am to do, I'll go crazy."

Just as Dr. King felt called by God to break the shackles of injustice, Coretta said, "I've been called by God, too." Martin noted the evidence. In his powerless moments like bombings, jail, and witnessing Coretta in childbirth, Coretta's divine strength kept his life in orbit.

Dr. King leaned on Coretta's prayers in the spring of 1963 when under his guidance the Southern Christian Leadership Conference (SCLC) organized "Project Confrontation" in Birmingham, Alabama. Project workshops trained adults to organize mass protests in opposition to segregation and Birmingham's refusal to hire Black workers in retail jobs. At that time, Birmingham was notorious for city leaders like Bull Connor, the commissioner of public safety, who supported white supremacy and violence.

When Black children joined the project to raise America's awareness of racial inequality, Connor ordered officers to attack them with fire hoses and police dogs. Loads of children were arrested and filled city jail cells. Because they wanted first-class citizenship more than convenience, dirty jail conditions did not discourage them.

Coretta and Martin stood amazed as minors showed a major display of soul force and moral power. Black children changed American history. After students packed the jail and Birmingham was persecuted across international news, city officials surrendered to the demands of Birmingham's Black community. The city agreed to desegregate stores, hire Black clerks, and drop all charges against the schoolchildren.

The Birmingham victory inspired President Kennedy to propose a civil rights bill that would fully integrate Black people into American society. The victory also moved Dr. King and major civil rights groups to organize the March on Washington for Jobs and Freedom. A march on Washington would demonstrate that discrimination in schools, employment, and housing needed to be abolished across the entire nation.

Coretta told Martin, "I believe one hundred thousand people would come to the nation's capital at your invitation." She miscalculated. When Dr. King called Americans to Washington on August 28, 1963, 250,000 raised banners demanding justice. The interracial assembly sent a loud message. Liberty was due to every American.

As Coretta and the crowd prepared to hear Dr. King, the last speaker for that day, singer Mahalia Jackson called across the stage, "Tell them about the dream, Martin!"

Dr. King improvised his famous speech like a jazz musician. Under Martin's thunder, the crowd cheered and Coretta watched the heavens open.

"*I have a dream that one day this nation will rise up and live out the true meaning of its creed: 'We hold these truths to be self-evident; that all men are created equal.'*"

1964

Nothing prepared Coretta for Kennedy's murder in '63.
Officers captured and accused Lee Harvey Oswald.
Bloodshed did not dash Coretta's hope for 1964.
Equal rights inspired her Freedom Concert tours.
Liberty for the lowly was the message in her music.

President Lyndon B. Johnson grieved the trying times.
Equal rights and Dr. King made demands on his soul.
America shined when Johnson raised a pen to sign the
Civil Rights Act of 1964! The bill abolished segregation.
Equality in schools, jobs, and housing was now the law.

People across the globe praised the changes in America.
RING! RING! Coretta answered the phone—always pleasant.
It was big news . . . Dr. King WON the 1964 Nobel Peace Prize.
Zeal and exhilaration zipped weary Martin to a starlit zenith.
Exhilaration and zeal put a smile on Coretta's face.

Freedom Road

Coretta and Martin had arrived at a mutual agreement by 1965. They both committed time to the movement and their growing children. Coretta served in the home and during Freedom Concerts she sang on stage to raise money for the Southern Christian Leadership Conference (SCLC). Martin preached for a living to keep the family fed. As the leader of SCLC, he organized protests to uproot systemic racism, a deadly creeping vine and outgrowth of American slavery.

When the Civil Rights Act of 1964 abolished segregation and Jim Crow signs disappeared, most Blacks in the South were still disenfranchised—they were deprived of the right to vote. Without the ballot box, they had no voice in city, state, or federal elections.

In an effort to give Black Americans full voting rights, Dr. King and the SCLC held rallies in Alabama with student organizer John Lewis and the Student Nonviolent Coordinating Committee (SNCC) in 1965.

Before they took to the streets, Dr. King sensed death. He said, "Someone is going to get killed." His words rang true. A white segregationist shot Jimmie Lee Jackson, a nonviolent activist. Jackson's death fortified the voting rights movement. SCLC and SNCC turned their mass demonstration to Selma in Dallas County, Alabama.

As Martin planned a fifty-mile march from Selma to the state capital in Montgomery, Coretta flew across the West Coast on a five-city tour raising money for rallies. She tracked the movement on TV. Coretta trembled at the news on March 7, 1965. On what would become known as Bloody Sunday, with John Lewis leading the way, state troopers attacked six hundred marchers as they kneeled to pray on the Edmund Pettus Bridge.

Officers discharged tear gas and beat demonstrators with nightsticks. One officer hit John Lewis and fractured his skull, leaving a permanent scar.

Coretta called Martin in a state of panic. She made plans to end the tour and fly back home. Martin encouraged her to stay the course and keep to her cosmic calling.

He said, "You're making a contribution right where you are."

Several days later in Selma, the Ku Klux Klan killed the Rev. James Reeb, a white minister and member of the SCLC. The evil in Selma reaped a wave of national sympathy and strong support for voting rights.

President Lyndon B. Johnson announced, "It is all of us who must overcome the crippling legacy of bigotry and injustice." On August 6, 1965, he signed the Voting Rights Act to ensure voter protections for every American.

With Selma behind them, Martin turned his focus north to Chicago, Illinois. He aimed to eliminate inequities and despair in the belly of urban blight. Coretta understood his desire to expose racial bias in big cities beyond the South. However, Coretta refocused her concerns on Vietnam as she still agonized over the war, nuclear arms, and the death of innocent people. The conflict was now in its tenth year.

Coretta urged Martin to voice his contempt for the Vietnam War at church podiums, college lectures, and street protests. But for the longest time, on the subject of Vietnam, Martin sat in silence. Coretta did not poke, push, or pout. She knew the soul behind the silence. When the fire in Martin's bones could no longer be contained, he would raise his voice on the side of peace.

1966

The Kings move up North
Coretta does not grimace
She is committed
Her support buoys Martin
Chicago needs his movement

The Kings have a plan
Drag evil into the light
Chi-town city blight
Busted windows and garbage
Hiding under piles of snow

Coretta hangs drapes
The family moves to Lawndale
Rats run the building
White slumlords collect the rent
Ignore Black tenant requests

Coretta hums hymns
Lawndale reeks with great despair
The North is the South
Blackness is perceived a crime
Black need is denied always

Sweet home Chicago
The Kings stay less than a year
Paltry "promised land"
They proclaim the Golden Rule
Their message is not received

Coretta looks blue
Little birds whisper rumors
Death is at her door
The movement demands martyrs
The grave beckons her true love

Down by the Riverside

The Kings left Chicago and settled back in Atlanta January, 1967. Coretta waited patiently on Martin. She hoped for a day when he would preach a pro-peace sermon and encourage America to end the Vietnam War. It was her opinion the Vietnam War drained monies that American children needed for schools and education.

During her waiting season, Coretta cared for her family, sang at Freedom Concerts, and marched in peace rallies. Then it happened on April 4, 1967. Venus and Saturn converged. Martin made Coretta's wish come true.

In the pulpit at Riverside Church in New York City, Martin joined the Clergy and Laymen Concerned About Vietnam. Surrounded by stained glass windows with crowded church pews before him, he pleaded with America to *study war no more*.

As he denounced the carnage of war, calling it "tragic," reporters said "Beyond Vietnam" was the most controversial speech in Dr. King's career. In the eyes of many, his criticism of America's participation in Vietnam made him appear unpatriotic.

Dr. King understood that speaking against the war would ruin some friendships and harden his enemies. He accepted the backlash and loudly proclaimed, "I have moved to break the betrayal of my own silences and to speak from the burnings of my heart."

At night as he slept in bed, Coretta studied Martin's face. His pro-peace message made her proud to be his earthly companion. There. He said it. Peace and nonviolence are Gemini twins. Martin spoke his truth at Riverside Church.

In the weeks and months after Martin's Vietnam speech, Coretta endured constant crank calls in their home. Callers did not whisper like chirping birds. They cackled loudly like witches. Angry anonymous voices called for Martin's death.

1968

March 28, 1968 . . . left a trail of tears, trash, and broken glass.
Every American city turned an eye toward Memphis, Tennessee.
Mayor Loeb denied fair wages to striking sanitation workers.
"Pass me not! O, gentle Savior," sang the Rev. James Lawson.
He called his old friend Martin during a strike strategy meeting.
In a few days—Martin visited Memphis to help the striking men.
Shots and shouts pierced the sky . . . Dr. King died April 4, 1968.

Brokenhearted Coretta gussied up her gloom in black radiance.
Life's tragedy left Venus alone to shine and pave a path for peace.
Underneath pain was a holy fire . . . Coretta preached in Memphis.
Entertainers, clergy, and marching men received her fiery admonitions.
She did more than sing a song . . . Coretta spoke truth to power.

Life after Death

When Coretta was a child, she heard men say, "Let the women be silent." In 1963 when she marched on Washington with Martin, Coretta remembered how men in the movement made room for Mahalia Jackson to sing. The same men did not make space that day for women and activists like Rosa Parks to speak weighty speeches and share their dreams about the future.

Just like Mahalia with her golden Gospel tunes, Coretta did more singing than speaking when Martin was alive. There comes an end to every season. During Coretta's life after Martin's death, she put away music to deliver freedom speeches in city parks, the Congress, and Ivy League colleges. Her lectures denounced racism, homophobia, poverty, and war. Coretta Scott King was the first woman to give the Class Day address at Harvard University in 1968.

Three priorities consumed Coretta after Martin died. She devoted care to her four children as a working single mother. She formed the King Center in Atlanta to teach nonviolence as a way to peaceful living. Last, but not the least, she worked with American leaders to make Dr. King's birth date a national holiday.

So many thought it was impossible to establish a holiday in honor of a Black man whose forefathers were enslaved. Coretta believed in miracles. She leaned on the faith that fueled her strength when faced with fires, bombings, and the Reidsville penitentiary.

From 1968 to 1979, Coretta pressed the American House and Senate to pass a holiday bill to commemorate Dr. King's life as an emblem of peace.

A friend asked Coretta, "Do you really believe we're going to get a holiday?" The odds were unlikely when Congress voted down the bill in 1979. Coretta was not dismayed. She assured her friend, "Yes, we will."

From 1979 to 1983, Coretta flew across the nation speaking with governors and mayors in her effort to gain support for a King holiday. She was indefatigable. Coretta Scott King launched a petition drive that resulted in six million signatures. She also organized a coalition of 750 political, religious, labor, and civil rights groups. They stood with Coretta when she testified before the Senate and Congress to express all the noble reasons her husband deserved to be honored for his sacrificial life.

On October 19, 1983, the Senate voted 78 to 22 to make Dr. King's birth date a national holiday. After fifteen years of lobbying, speaking, writing, and waiting, Coretta reached the zenith of her impossible dream. The King bill was the first national holiday established to honor someone other than Christopher Columbus or a US president.

On November 3, 1983, Coretta and the King children, supported by members of their extended family, joined an array of political leaders in Washington, DC. There in the famous Rose Garden, Coretta watched as President Ronald Reagan signed the King holiday into law. It was established that the holiday would be celebrated on the third Monday of January, beginning in 1986.

Coretta Scott King used her voice to preserve the memory and legacy of Dr. King's life. She stood up and spoke out. Certain men who marched with Martin told her to sit and not say a word. They did not understand the power at work. Coretta was a Scott. She was Obadiah's seed and shrinking was a sin. There was a cosmic mandate on her life. Coretta answered the call.

2006

Ebenezer Church
Winter raindrops fell like tears
Four Kings bowed to pray
Blues hymns eased their bitter grief
Jesus called Coretta home

Timeline

1927   Coretta is born on April 27.

1953   Marries Martin Luther King Jr. on June 18.

1954   The couple moves to Montgomery, Alabama.
Martin pastors at Dexter Avenue Baptist Church.

1955   First child, Yolanda, born on November 17.

Montgomery bus boycott begins on December 5.

1956   The King home is bombed on January 30.

Montgomery bus boycott ends on December 20.
US Supreme Court outlaws segregation on city buses.

1957   Second child, Martin III, born on October 23.

Coretta travels to Ghana with Martin to celebrate
independence from Great Britain.

1959   Spends a month with Martin in India studying Gandhi's
techniques of nonviolence as guests of Prime Minister Nehru.

1960   Coretta and Martin move their family to Atlanta, Georgia.

1961   Third child, Dexter, born on January 30.

1962   Coretta travels to Geneva, Switzerland, with Women Strike
for Peace to protest nuclear testing and the Vietnam War.

1963   Fourth child, Bernice "Bunny," born on March 28.

1964–65   Coretta performs a series of Freedom Concerts to raise
money for the Southern Christian Leadership Conference (SCLC).

Coretta Scott King, 1964

The wedding of Martin Luther King Jr. and
Coretta Scott, June 18, 1953

1968	Martin is assassinated in Memphis, Tennessee, on the balcony of the Lorraine Motel, on April 4.
	Coretta leads a silent march of 40,000 people through the streets of Memphis on April 8.
	The next day in Atlanta, Georgia, she makes a televised speech at her husband's funeral on April 9. Coretta establishes the King Memorial Center in Atlanta on June 26.
	She is the first woman to deliver the Class Day address at Harvard University.
1974	Develops the Full Employment Action Council, dedicated to national policy for full employment and equal economic opportunity.
1979	Testifies before joint hearings of Congress in support of a national holiday honoring Dr. King.
1982	Forms the Coalition of Conscience, a group of 750 human rights organizations to support the campaign for a King holiday and sponsor the twentieth anniversary of the March on Washington.
1983	Lobbies the Congress to establish a King holiday.
	President Reagan signs King Holiday bill into law on November 3.
1986	First national celebration of the King Holiday on January 20.
1990	Coretta cohosts the Soviet-American Women's Summit in Washington, DC.
1995	Steps down as chief executive officer of the King Center.
2002	Visits the White House on the King holiday—January 21.
2004	Mrs. King and President George W. Bush lay a wreath at Dr. King's tomb on what would have been his seventy-fifth birthday, January 15.
2006	Coretta battles cancer and passes away on January 30.
	She lies in repose on Auburn Avenue in Atlanta at the historic Ebenezer Baptist Church on February 6. More than 100,000 mourners gather to pay their final respects.
	Funeral services are held in Atlanta on February 7.

Author's Note

Who is Coretta Scott King? Many readers know her as the wife and widow of Dr. Martin Luther King Jr. She is an iconic image dressed in a sheer black veil on the cover of *Life* magazine in 1968. I wrote this book to introduce readers to the woman behind the veil. With spunk and pluck, Coretta Scott King was a drum major for justice.

Without Coretta's influence, it is possible Dr. King would not have stood so resolutely to abolish legal segregation on the Freedom Highway. It is certain that without Coretta's prophetic preachments after his death, Martin's name would be a faint memory.

Coretta worked tirelessly to honor Dr. King with a federal holiday. And wherever she was given a platform to speak, she encouraged listeners to employ Dr. King's nonviolent direct action as a way of life. Nonviolence, she said, is more than a tactic for freedom crusades. It is a high road toward personal peace and human solidarity.

My text leans heavily on imagery and metaphor connected to the cosmos and celestial objects. There is a reason for this. Coretta and Martin believed their marriage and the calling on their lives to be divinely appointed—beyond earthly perimeters. Coretta and Martin called God a "cosmic companion." Therefore, when Coretta did find herself a widow, her feet did not stray off the Freedom Highway. It was her opinion that a cosmic companion strengthened her will and spirited her feet to keep on marching.

Dr. and Mrs. King, 1964

Coretta Scott King speaks at an event in which a time capsule holding some of Dr. King's possessions is lowered into the ground at Freedom Plaza in Washington, DC, 1988.

Bibliography

All quotations used in the book can be found in the following sources marked with an asterisk (*).

*Bagley, Edythe Scott, and Joseph H. Hilley. *Desert Rose: The Life and Legacy of Coretta Scott King*. Tuscaloosa: University of Alabama Press, 2012.

Bennett, Lerone. *What Manner of Man: A Biography of Martin Luther King, Jr.* Chicago: Johnson Publishing Co., 1968.

Carson, Clayborne, Ralph E. Luker, and Penny A. Russell, editors. *The Papers of Martin Luther King, Jr., Vol. 1, Called to Serve, January 1929–June 1951*. Berkeley: University of California Press, 1992.

Fernandez, Benedict J. *Countdown to Eternity: Photographs of Dr. Martin Luther King, Jr. in the 1960s*. Rochester, New York: Manchester Craftsmens Guild, 1993.

Gelfand, Dale Evva, and Lisa Renee Rhodes. *Coretta Scott King: Civil Rights Activist*. New York: Chelsea House, 2007.

King, Bernice A. Phone interview, March 15, 2018.

*King, Coretta Scott, and Barbara A. Reynolds. *My Life, My Love, My Legacy*. New York: Henry Holt and Company, 2017.

*King, Martin Luther, Jr. *A Testament of Hope: The Essential Writings and Speeches of Martin Luther King, Jr.* Edited by James Melvin Washington. New York: HarperOne, 2006.

———. *The Words of Martin Luther King, Jr.* Selected by Coretta Scott King. New York: William Morrow, 2014.

*"The South: Attack on the Conscience." *Time*, February 18, 1957: 17–20.

Theoharis, Jeanne. *A More Beautiful and Terrible History: The Uses and Misuses of Civil Rights History*. Boston: Beacon Press, 2018.

*Vivian, Octavia B. *Coretta: The Story of Mrs. Martin Luther King, Jr.* Philadelphia: Fortress Press, 1970.

Text Credits

The Selma to Montgomery March, 1965. From left: Dr. Ralph Abernathy, Dr. King's best friend; Rev. James Reeb; the Abernathy children; and Dr. and Mrs. King.

In memory of Mary Louise Stamper Powell —*AFD*

To the King family and for all the civil right heroes
who deserved to be well known —*RGC*

Acknowledgments

Dr. Martin Luther King Jr. captured my imagination during childhood. Books about the leader felt so personal and alive that I told my second-grade teacher, "Dr. King is a friend of mine." Forty years later, in 2017, I read Coretta Scott King's autobiography. Mrs. King's memories were so palpable that I went on a journey to research Coretta, the fearless "drum major for justice," who was overlooked during my early education. While she was challenged by racial terror as a child, I found that Coretta Scott King was raised by parents who gave her the tools and permission to live her grandest dreams. The Scotts served as models of courage. It is that courage that Coretta offered Martin as they marched for freedom during the American Civil Rights Movement. How many children and adults miss Coretta's conquering fire as they are mesmerized by Martin's light? Mrs. King was more than a pretty wife and doting mother. She was an unwavering activist. Upon Martin's death, she used her voice like a prophet speaking truth to power. In the process of writing this book I encountered a great spirit whose wisdom is a guiding light—even now. And I am grateful. Coretta Scott King is a friend of mine.

Picture Credits

Alpha Historica / Alamy Stock Photo: 47; Bridgeman Images: 44 (bottom); Library of Congress: 2008677732: 44 (top), 96516151: 46 (top), 2011632686: 46 (bottom).

Text copyright © 2023 by Alice Faye Duncan • Illustrations copyright © 2023 by R. Gregory Christie

Calkins Creek • An imprint of Astra Books for Young Readers, a division of Astra Publishing House • astrapublishinghouse.com • Printed in China

ISBN: 978-1-6626-8004-5 (hc) • ISBN: 978-1-6626-8005-2 (eBook) • Library of Congress Control Number: 2021925703

First edition
10 9 8 7 6 5 4 3 2 1

Design by Barbara Grzeslo • The text is set in Frutiger Concensed. • The titles are set in Frutiger Bold Concensed.
The illustrations are done in mixed media watercolor.